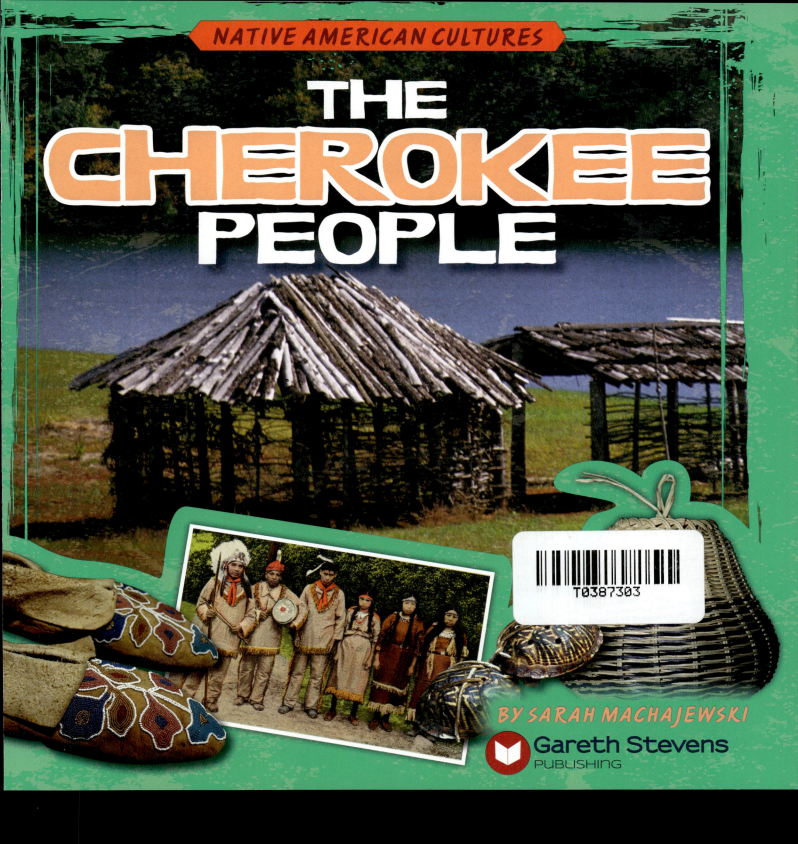

Please visit our website, www.garethstevens.com. For a free color catalog of all our high-quality books, call toll free 1-800-542-2595 or fax 1-877-542-2596.

Library of Congress Cataloging-in-Publication Data

Machajewski, Sarah.
 The Cherokee people / Sarah Machajewski.
      pages cm — (Native American cultures)
 Includes bibliographical references and index.
 ISBN 978-1-4824-1977-1 (pbk.)
 ISBN 978-1-4824-1978-8 (6 pack)
 ISBN 978-1-4824-1979-5 (library binding)
 1. Cherokee Indians—Juvenile literature. I. Title.
 E99.C5M28 2015
 975.004'97557—dc23

2014021932

First Edition

Published in 2015 by
Gareth Stevens Publishing
111 East 14th Street, Suite 349
New York, NY 10003

Copyright © 2015 Gareth Stevens Publishing

Designer: Sarah Liddell
Editor: Therese Shea

Photo credits: Cover, pp. 1 (main image, turtle rattles, basket), 11, 13, 15 Marilyn Angel Wynn/ Nativestock/Getty Images; cover, p. 1 (moccasins) Daderot/Wikimedia Commons; cover, p. 1 (corn dancers) Culture Club/Contributor/Hulton Archive/Getty Images; p. 5 LAWRENCE MIGDALE/Photo Researchers/Getty Images; p. 7 Ævar Arnfjörð Bjarmason/Wikimedia Commons; pp. 9, 25 Rainer Lesniewski/Shutterstock.com; p. 17 Robfergusonjr/Wikimedia Commons; p. 19 Apic/Contributor/Hulton Archive/Getty Images; p. 20 Tungsten/Wikimedia Commons; p. 21 Nesnad/Wikimedia Commons; p. 23 photo courtesy of the Library of Congress; p. 27 Education Images/UIG/Universal Images Group/Getty Images; p. 29 BotMultichillT/Wikimedia Commons.

All rights reserved. No part of this book may be reproduced in any form without permission in writing from the publisher, except by a reviewer.

Printed in the United States of America

CPSIA compliance information: Batch #CW15GS: For further information contact Gareth Stevens, New York, New York at 1-800-542-2595.

CONTENTS

Meet the Cherokee 4

North America's First People 6

The Beginning of the Cherokee Nation . . . 8

Cherokee Homes 10

Raising the "Three Sisters" 12

Cherokee Society 14

The White Man in North America 16

The Battle for Land Begins 18

Changing the Cherokee Culture 20

The White Man Takes Over 22

The Trail of Tears 24

Rebuilding a Nation 26

The Cherokee of Today 28

Glossary 30

For More Information 31

Index 32

Words in the glossary appear in **bold** type the first time they are used in the text.

MEET THE CHEROKEE

The Cherokee are a Native American tribe. Their story goes back thousands of years, long before the United States was a country. This history is one of **tradition**, courage, struggle, and a remarkable ability to overcome hardship.

Today, the Cherokee tribe is the largest native tribe in the United States. Outside the tribe, many people proudly claim they have Cherokee **ancestors**. Studying Cherokee **culture** of the past and present can teach us a lot about one of America's original people.

This mother and daughter practice sewing like their Cherokee ancestors did hundreds of years ago.

5

NORTH AMERICA'S FIRST PEOPLE

The history of the Cherokee people begins with the history of all native people. Native Americans are people whose ancestors settled in North America about 15,000 years ago. They may have crossed into North America from Asia using a land bridge.

Groups of people slowly moved south to areas where they could find food. They settled in different places. Over time, they lost contact with each other. That's how separate tribes, such as the Cherokee, formed their own societies.

DID YOU KNOW?

Before the Europeans arrived with horses, the Cherokee traveled by foot or by canoe.

The land bridge native people may have used is now covered with water. It's called the Bering Strait. At one time, it was dry enough for people to walk across.

THE BEGINNING OF THE CHEROKEE NATION

The Cherokee's ancestors settled in the Appalachian Mountains in what is now the southeastern United States. Their villages were on land that later became Kentucky, West Virginia, Virginia, North Carolina, South Carolina, Georgia, Alabama, and Tennessee. Today, most Cherokee people live in Oklahoma. Some live on a **reservation** in North Carolina.

The Creek, another native tribe, may have given the Cherokee their name. "Cherokee" may be from a Creek word meaning "people of different speech." However, many Cherokee people call themselves *aniyvwiya*, which means "real people."

DID YOU KNOW?

Cherokee legend says a water beetle dove to the bottom of the sea and brought mud back up to the surface. The mud spread out and created Earth.

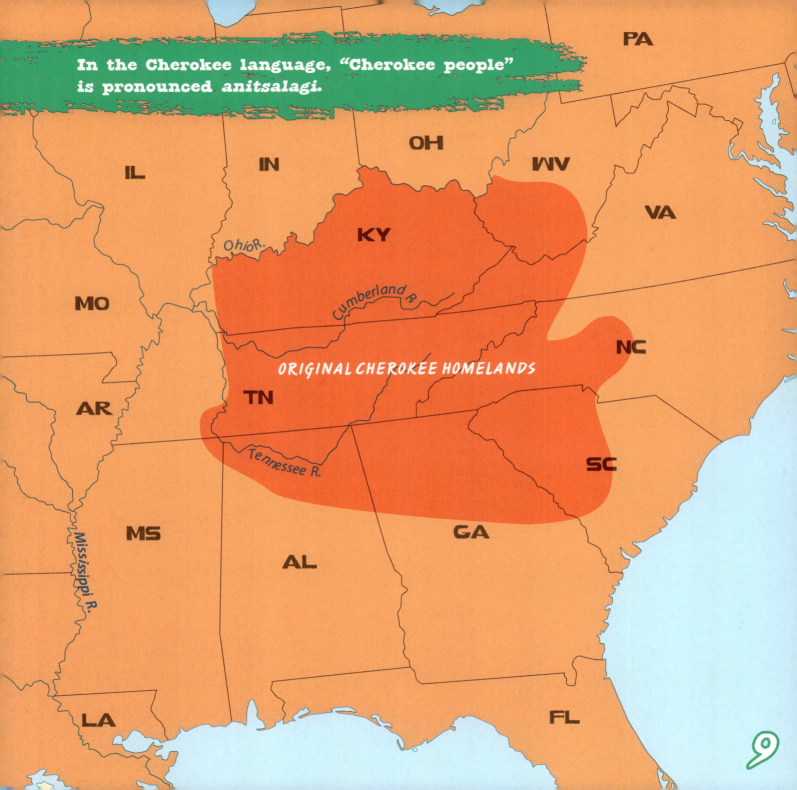

CHEROKEE HOMES

Early Cherokee lived in houses constructed of mud and clay. The roofs were made of grass and branches. These homes were permanent, which meant families stayed in the same spot all year long. Villages formed as more homes were built.

Today's Cherokee people live in homes like the ones found in your neighborhood. Many live on reservations. Reservations are independent communities governed by Native Americans. They have houses, schools, businesses, parks, and more.

DID YOU KNOW?

A traditional Cherokee village had between 30 and 60 homes. Each village had a council house where meetings and important events were held.

This photo shows what an early Cherokee home looked like.

RAISING THE "THREE SISTERS"

Villages formed in areas where food was easy to grow or find. The Cherokee grew large amounts of corn, beans, and squash. These crops are known as the "three sisters" because they were so important to many natives, including the Cherokee, and grew well together.

The Cherokee hunted wild animals. They also gathered nuts, berries, and roots from forests. These were used to make soups, cornbread, and more. Many of today's Cherokee celebrate their **heritage** by preparing and eating the foods their ancestors ate.

DID YOU KNOW?

The Cherokee's traditional Green Corn Ceremony was celebrated when the first corn ripened. The celebration included playing sports, fasting, praying, and performing special dances.

This basket contains traditional Cherokee foods, like squash, beans, and nuts.

CHEROKEE SOCIETY

In early Cherokee society, the men were the hunters and warriors. Women farmed, cared for their families, wove baskets, and made pottery. Each Cherokee village had a chief.

The Cherokee people had **rituals** that honored different parts of their lives. The Cherokee stomp dance is a ritual that's still practiced today. It honors the Cherokee Creator God, Unetlanv. The stomp dance is performed around a special fire. Dancers called "shell-shakers" wear noisemaking objects around their legs. The noise helps keep the rhythm of the dance.

DID YOU KNOW?

In today's stomp dances, shell-shakers may wear pebble-filled cans.

This photo shows the turtle shells that early Cherokee shell-shakers wore during the stomp dance. Filling the turtle shells with pebbles created noise as the dancer moved around.

THE WHITE MAN IN NORTH AMERICA

The Cherokee's culture was left alone for hundreds of years until the 1600s, when large numbers of Europeans came to settle in North America. England formed several colonies where the Cherokee lived. This changed the Cherokee way of life forever.

The Cherokee began trading with the British in the 1600s. Cherokee exchanged animal furs for European guns, pots, knives, and other tools. These made parts of the Cherokee's lives easier, but it also changed some of their traditional ways.

DID YOU KNOW?

In 1540, Spanish explorer Hernando de Soto was the first European to make contact with the Cherokee.

A British artist made this drawing of three Cherokee men in the 1700s.

THE BATTLE FOR LAND BEGINS

After white settlers colonized North American territory, they believed the land belonged to them—even though natives had lived there long before them. Many settlers also viewed Native Americans as **uncivilized**, so they treated them unfairly.

The Cherokee realized how much their lives had changed since white settlers came to their land. Many believed **assimilating** into white culture would make the white population view the Cherokee as equals. They hoped it would make the whites treat them with respect.

DID YOU KNOW?

The American colonies declared their independence from England in 1776. The Cherokee were forced to give up much of their land as the Americans and British fought for territory.

One way the Cherokee assimilated was by changing the kinds of homes they lived in. They began living in log cabins instead of their traditional mud homes.

CHANGING THE CHEROKEE CULTURE

Besides their homes, the Cherokee people changed their appearance as they assimilated. Traditionally, the Cherokee wore animal skins, beaded belts, and moccasins on their feet. By the end of the 1700s, most had given these up for the pants, jackets, dresses, skirts, and shoes white people wore.

Cherokee society also changed greatly. The tribe formed a government modeled after the United States government and even had a **constitution**. The Cherokee practiced white **religions** and created schools, too.

SEQUOYAH

DID YOU KNOW?

In 1821, a Cherokee man named Sequoyah (seh-KWOY-ah) created the Cherokee syllabary, a writing system. Almost the entire tribe learned how to read and write.

ᏣᎳᎩ ᏧᎴᎯᏌᏅᎯ

CHEROKEE PHOENIX.

VOL. I. NEW ECHOTA, WEDNESDAY MAY 21, 1828. **NO. 13.**

EDITED BY ELIAS BOUDINOTT
PRINTED WEEKLY BY
ISAAC H. HARRIS,
FOR THE CHEROKEE NATION.

At $2.50 if paid in advance, $3 in six months, or $3.50 if paid at the end of the year.

To subscribers who can read only the Cherokee language the price will be $2,00 in advance, or $2,50 to be paid within the year.

Every subscription will be considered as continued unless subscribers give notice to the contrary before the commencement of a new year.

Any person procuring six subscribers, and becoming responsible for the payment, shall receive a seventh gratis.

Advertisements will be inserted at seventy-five cents per square for the first insertion, and thirty-seven and a half cents for each continuance; longer ones in proportion.

☞ All letters addressed to the Editor, post paid, will receive due attention.

AGENTS FOR THE CHEROKEE PHOENIX.

The following persons are authorized to receive subscriptions and payments for the Cherokee Phoenix.

HENRY HILL, Esq. Treasurer of the A. B. F. M. Boston, Mass.
GEORGE M. TRACY, Agent of the A. B. New York.
Rev. A. D. EDDY, Canandaigua, N. Y.
WILLARD & CONVERSE, Richmond, Va.
Rev. JAMES CAMPBELL, Beaufort, S. C.
Mr. GEORGE SMITH, Statesville, W. T.
Mr. BENNET ROBERTS—Powal Me.
Rev. THOS. R. GOLD, an itinerant Gentleman.

CHEROKEE LAWS.

New Town, Nov. 10, 1825.

Resolved by the National Committee and Council, That the children of Cherokee men and white women, living in the Cherokee nation as man and wife, be, and they are hereby acknowledged to be equally entitled to all the immunities and privileges enjoyed by the citizens descending from the Cherokee race, by the mother's side.

By order of the National Committee,
JNO. ROSS, Pres't N. Committee.
MAJOR RIDGE, Speaker.
his
PATH ⋈ KILLER.
mark.
CHARLES HICKS.
A. M'COY, Clerk of the N. Com.
E. BOUDINOTT, Clk. N. Coun.

New Town, Nov. 10, 1824.

Resolved by the National Committee and Council, That the section embraced in the law regulating marriages between white men and Cherokee women, and making it unlawful for white men to have more than one wife and recommending all others also to have but one wife, be, and the same is hereby amended, so that it shall not be lawful hereafter, for any person or persons whatsoever, to have more than one wife.

By order of the N. Committee,
JNO. ROSS, Pres't N. Com.
MAJOR RIDGE, Speaker.
his
Approved—PATH ⋈ KILLER.
A. M'COY, Clerk, National Com.
E. BOUDINOTT, Clk. N. Council

New Town, Nov. 10, 1825.

Resolved by the National Committee and Council, That a fence of four inches crack between each rail, for two and a half feet up from the ground, shall be considered a lawful fence, and the hogs of any person or persons whatsoever, breaking into the field of a person having such a fence, the owner or owners of such property shall be responsible for all the damages sustained, and the courts of the several districts shall have jurisdiction thereof; which may be left by any person or persons removing to another place, and the improvements so left, remain unoccupied for the term of three years, such improvements shall be considered abandoned, and any other person or persons, whatsoever, may take and go in possession of such improvements, in the same manner as if there were no improvements.

By order of the N. Committee,
JNO. ROSS, Pres't. Nat. Com.
his
PATH ⋈ KILLER.
mark.
A. M'COY, Clerk N. Com.
E. BOUDINOTT, Clerk of N. Council.

New Town, Nov. 12, 1825.

Resolved by the National Committee and Council, That all lawful contracts shall be binding, and whenever judgments shall have been obtained from any of the courts of justice in the Cherokee nation, against any person or persons whatsoever, on a plea of debt, it shall be lawful for such judgment or judgments by giving bond with sufficient security within five days after such judgment shall have been issued; and the stay shall not exceed for all sums under ten dollars, twenty days; for all sums from ten and under thirty dollars, sixty days; for all sums from thirty and under fifty dollars, ninety days; for all sums from fifty dollars and under one hundred, six months; and for all sums over one hundred dollars, nine months; and in case the person or persons against whom judgment or judgments shall be issued to give bond and security as aforesaid, it shall be the duty of the officer or officers, in whose hands such judgment or judgments may be placed, to levy upon his, her or their property, and advertise the same for public sale. For all sums from one to one hundred dollars, ten days; for all sums over one hundred and fifty, twenty days; for all sums over two hundred and fifty dollars, thirty days indulgence shall be given for the redemption of all such property sold agreeably to their official authorities. All sums over the amount of the debt for which the property is sold after deducting

---

[Cherokee syllabary columns]

CORRESPONDENCE,
Between Geos. Gray, Davidson and Cocke, late Commissioners of the United States, and Messrs. John Ross and Ridge, on the part of the Cherokee Nation.

[CONTINUED.]

The Cherokee published the first Native American newspaper, the Cherokee Phoenix, in 1828. It was published in English and the Cherokee language.

THE WHITE MAN TAKES OVER

Despite the Cherokee's efforts to assimilate, the white population still wanted the tribe's land. They wanted it even more after gold was discovered in Cherokee territory in Georgia.

Cherokee fought for their rights in the US Supreme Court, the highest court in the nation. The court decided Georgia had no rule over the Cherokee and couldn't claim their land. However, politicians pressured a small number of Cherokee into signing a treaty that sold land to the United States in 1835. Most Cherokee were unhappy with this decision.

A part white, part Cherokee man named John Ross fought for the Cherokee people to keep their land. He led them through hard times and later became an important chief of the Cherokee nation.

THE TRAIL OF TEARS

Andrew Jackson, the president of the United States, signed the Indian Removal Act of 1830 to make the Cherokee leave Georgia. He ignored the Supreme Court's decision that the Cherokee were a separate nation and sent 7,000 US troops into Cherokee territory.

In the winter of 1838–1839, the soldiers forced the Cherokee off their land. Cherokee men, women, and children marched more than 1,000 miles (1,609 km) to a special reservation in Oklahoma. Over 4,000 Cherokee died on the way. This march has become known as the "Trail of Tears."

DID YOU KNOW?

Many Cherokee were forced to march in the winter without proper shelter or clothing—sometimes without shoes. There wasn't enough food, and the Cherokee weren't allowed to stop or rest.

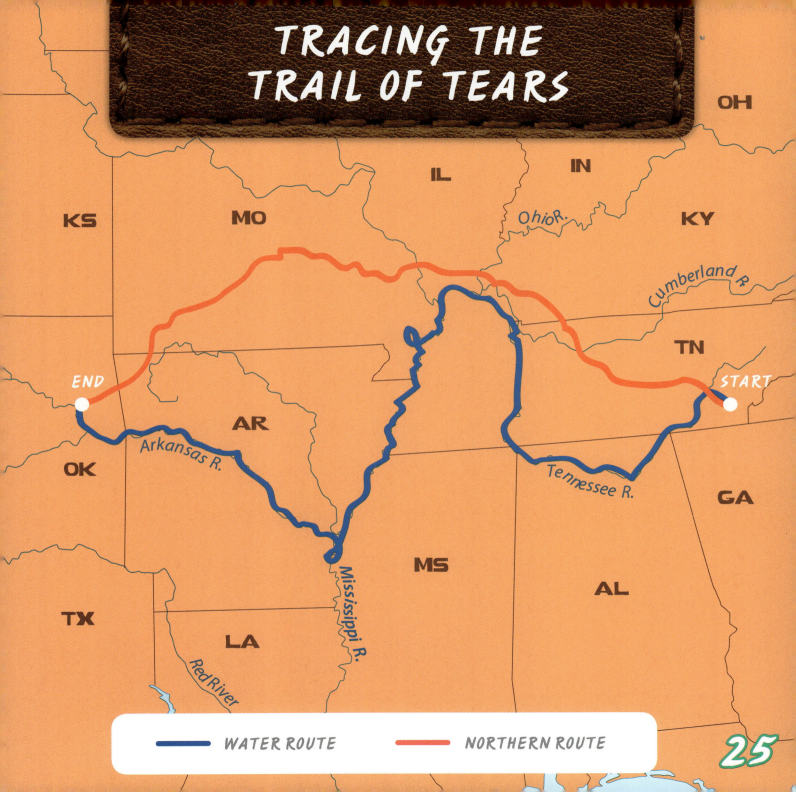

REBUILDING A NATION

The Trail of Tears brought great suffering to the Cherokee. The people lost land, family, and friends. There were years of unrest between Cherokee who had signed the 1835 treaty and those who had fought against it. It took many years to rebuild Cherokee society. However, courage helped the Cherokee recover.

Modern Cherokee have their own government, schools, and businesses. Some businesses earn millions of dollars. Many Cherokee have become successful politicians and artists. Cherokee children attend schools taught by Cherokee teachers, and many students go to college.

DID YOU KNOW?

A few hundred Cherokee escaped to the mountains before the Trail of Tears. Their descendants live in western North Carolina today.

The Museum of the Cherokee Indian is located in Cherokee, North Carolina. It's open to visitors year-round.

THE CHEROKEE OF TODAY

Today, there are three main Cherokee groups: the Cherokee Nation, the United Keetoowah Band of Cherokee Indians, and the Eastern Band of Cherokee Indians. The total number of citizens across all the Cherokee bands is around 350,000. About 126,000 citizens live on the Cherokee Nation's land in Oklahoma. People with Cherokee ancestry live all over the world.

Modern Cherokee have an important job. They work to keep their tribe successful while also carrying on their culture. By understanding and celebrating their past, they can build a strong and successful future.

Cherokee children learn about their heritage by taking part in ceremonies.

29

GLOSSARY

ancestor: a relative who lived long before you

assimilate: to blend in with another culture by adopting their ways of life

ceremony: an event to honor or celebrate something

constitution: a piece of writing that states the laws of a country or organization

culture: the beliefs and ways of life of a group of people

fast: to choose not to eat all or some kinds of food, especially for religious reasons

heritage: something that comes from past members of a family or group

religion: a belief in and way of honoring a god or gods

reservation: land set aside by the US government for Native Americans

ritual: a formal ceremony

tradition: a long-practiced custom

uncivilized: not having a high level of culture

FOR MORE INFORMATION

BOOKS

Benoit, Peter. *The Trail of Tears*. New York, NY: Children's Press, 2012.

De Capua, Sarah. *The Cherokee*. New York, NY: Marshall Cavendish Benchmark, 2006.

Wade, Mary Dodson. *Amazing Cherokee Writer Sequoyah*. Berkeley Heights, NJ: Enslow, 2010.

WEBSITES

Cherokee Nation
www.cherokee.org/Home.aspx
This is the official website of the Cherokee Nation, which provides information on the past and present of the Cherokee people.

Native American Facts for Kids
www.native-languages.org/kids.htm
This organization provides facts on many Native American tribes, including the Cherokee.

Publisher's note to educators and parents: Our editors have carefully reviewed these websites to ensure that they are suitable for students. Many websites change frequently, however, and we cannot guarantee that a site's future contents will continue to meet our high standards of quality and educational value. Be advised that students should be closely supervised whenever they access the Internet.

INDEX

ancestors 4, 5, 6, 8, 12

Appalachian Mountains 8

assimilating 18, 19, 20, 22

Cherokee Nation 28

Cherokee Phoenix 21

clothing 20

culture 4, 16, 18, 28

Eastern Band of Cherokee Indians 28

foods 12, 13

Georgia 8, 22, 24

Green Corn Ceremony 12

heritage 12, 29

homes 10, 11, 19, 20

Indian Removal Act of 1830 24

language 9

North Carolina 8, 26, 27

Oklahoma 8, 24, 28

reservation 8, 10, 24

rituals 14

Ross, John 23

Sequoyah 20

settlers 16, 18

society 14, 20, 26

stomp dance 14, 15

syllabary 20

Trail of Tears 24, 26

United Keetoowah Band of Cherokee Indians 28

villages 8, 10, 12, 14

NATIVE AMERICAN CULTURES

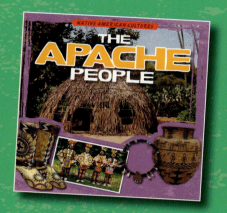

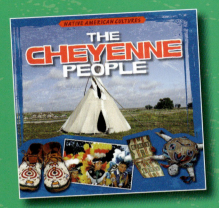

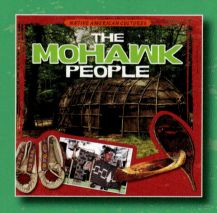
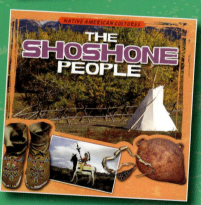

Levels: GR: N; DRA: 30

ISBN: 978-1-4824-1977-1
6-pack ISBN: 978-1-4824-1978-8

Gareth Stevens
PUBLISHING

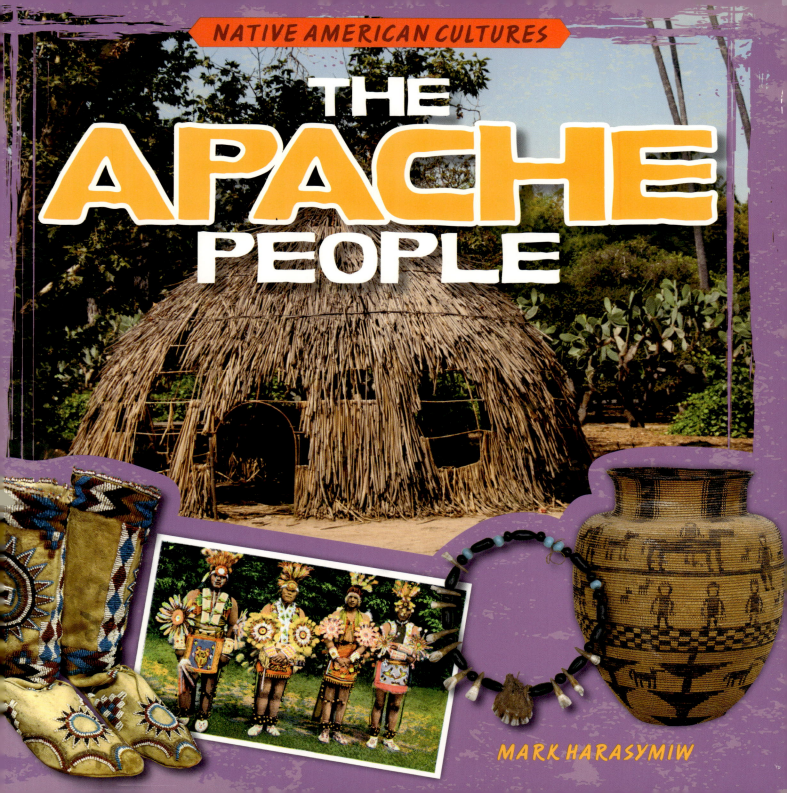